# NANCY ORTT

# ARIEL'S RESCUE

Balboa Press books may be ordered through booksellers or by contacting:

Balboa Press
A Division of Hay House
1663 Liberty Drive
Bloomington, IN 47403
www.balboapress.com
1 (877) 407-4847

Interior Graphics/Art Credit: Ashka Taylor

ISBN: 978-1-9822-1307-7 (sc)
ISBN: 978-1-9822-1308-4 (e)

Library of Congress Control Number: 2018911960

Print information available on the last page.

Balboa Press rev. date: 10/17/2018

BALBOA.
PRESS
A DIVISION OF HAY HOUSE

# Ariel's Rescue

Dear Cousins, Ava, Brian, Chris, Kayla, Kylie, Kaden, and Weston,

Mommy says I should tell you my story because when my mommy or your mommies referred to me as a rescue dog, you thought of dogs who rescue people.

There's all kinds of other rescue dogs. There's dogs who rescue people who have been buried under collapsed buildings, an' dogs who sniff out things that go BOOM!

There's dogs who rescue people from bumping into things. They are called Seeing Eye dogs. (Their mommies and daddies don't see so good, so they help out.)

My Aunt Tracey doesn't see so good, but she doesn't have one of them. She uses a cane to help her. Mommy says I have to watch out for Aunt Tracey's cane, 'cause Aunt Tracey can't watch out for me! I love Aunt Tracey. (I doesn't like her cane, though.)

I'm called a "Rescue Dog". Mommy says the words should be "Rescued Dog", but people don't put the D on the end. (Mommy is smart like that.) Now, I live with my Mommy and my Mom-mom...an' we love one another—LOTS!

...but it wasn't always that way in my life. A long, long time ago, I had a different family. They kept me outside ALL of the time! I like outside, but I like inside, too. Even when the weather was REALLY hot I was outside. (Have you noticed my fluffy fur?) Would you like to be outside all day in the summer time in a coat?"

Then, my family didn't love me anymore. I don't know why. My family told me that we were going for a ride. We went for a long, long ride. I had a good time on that ride. Then, we got out and I ran around and had fun...and they drove away without me! I was confused! I was hurt! Why would they do that? I loved my family.

I felt lost! I didn't know what to do. Some nice people would sometimes feed me nice-good food. Then, someone tried to feed me dirt. (Mommy says that's why now, I smell everything real good before I eat it).

I spent a long time without a family. Sometimes, I had to find my own dinner. Sometimes, I went hungry. I got all dirty and my pretty fur got matted.

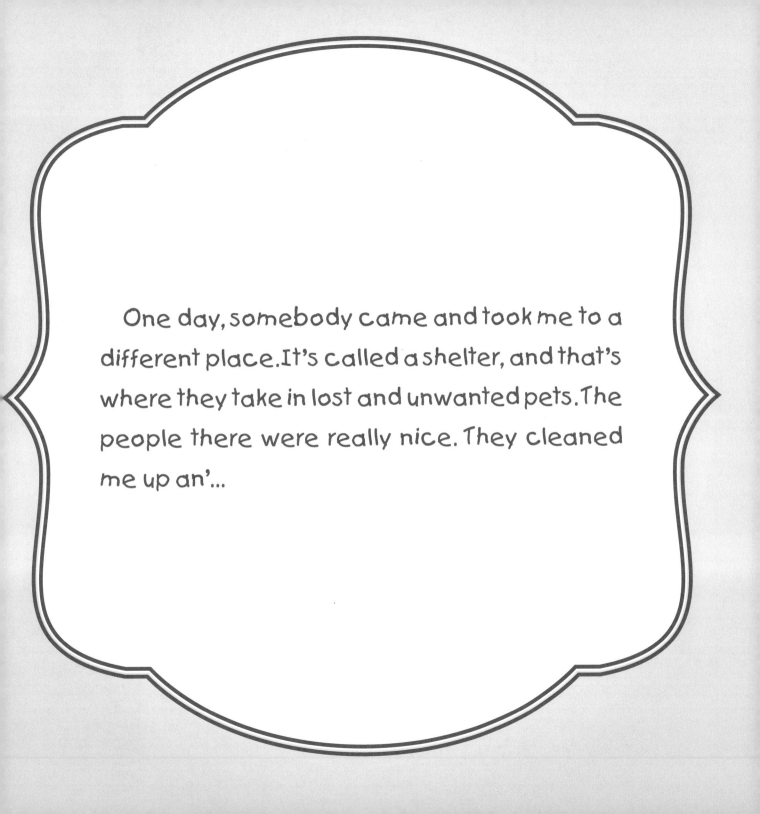

One day, somebody came and took me to a different place. It's called a shelter, and that's where they take in lost and unwanted pets. The people there were really nice. They cleaned me up an'...

...a doctor examined me. She told the shelter people that I had heart worms. You can't see them. They're on the inside. The doctor gave the shelter people medicine to get rid of the heart worms. She said that at one time I had puppies. I had a little operation, so I can't have puppies anymore. I'm not sad. I loved my puppies, but it's a lot of responsibility taking care of them. Mommy an' Mom-mom say I am a little girl, an' I don't need all that responsibility.

One of the shelter ladies called Eskie Rescuers United American Eskimo Dog Rescue, (cause I'm mostly an American Eskimo Dog). My soon-to-be foster mom came for me. She took me home where I learned how to be a good girl inside...and, I had fur-siblings! Oh was that fun!

I stayed there for a few months before Mommy, Mom-mom, and Aunt Sue came for me. I was happy when they came. But I didn't like the ride. That's how Mommy and Aunt Sue figured I had been taken for a ride and abandon. The longer we were in Mommy's van the scareder I got. I was shaking really bad—I was so scared that I threw up twice. It was a long ride. Mommy, and Aunt Sue drove all day to take me home!

When I finally got in my new yard, I went ZOOMIES! ZOOMIES! ZOOMIES!!! I ran lots! I smelled my new yard. There were lots of good smells!

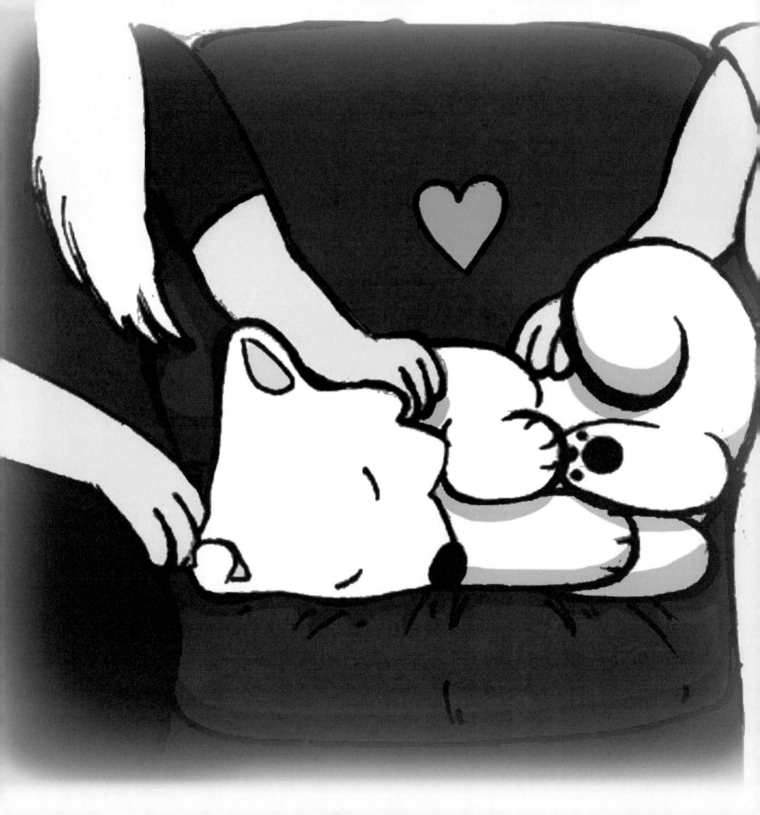

Inside, Mommy fed me and gave me water. Aunt Sue went home. I explored my new house. Mommy and Mom-mom showed me my new toys and my new bed. I didn't sleep in my bed that night, I slept with Mommy. She let me sleep on her bed! The shelter people, Eskie Rescue, Mommy, Aunt Sue, an' Mom-mom rescued me from a bad life. An' we live happily ever after! Mommy even gives me birthday parties! (But, that's another story!)

# About the Author

Nancy has been a natural teacher all of her life. She has loved or owned dogs for as long as she can remember. Nancy is an educational enthusiast who loves to share her knowledge. At one point, she specialized in teaching people with special needs. She is currently Aunt Nance to a second generation of nieces and nephews.

Ariel is a happy, full-of-love girl, who likes going for coffee with Mommy and Mom-mom. She also loves tummy rubs.

Printed in the United States
By Bookmasters